THE INDIAN LANDSCAPES AND NATURE

AN EXPLORATION OF INDIA'S NATURAL BEAUTY AND DIVERSITY

DR. JAGADEESH PILLAI

Made with ♥ on the Notion Press Platform
www.notionpress.com

|| Dedicated to all wisdom seekers around the world ||

ℵ

Contents

Contents

PRAYER

"Om Bhadram Karnebhih Shrunuyaama DevaahBhadram Pashyemaakshabhiryajatraah Sthirairangaistushtuvaamsastanoobhih Vyashema Devahitam YadaayuhSwasti Na Indro VridhashravaahSwasti Nah Pooshaa VishwavedaahSwasti Nastaarkshyo ArishtanemihSwasti No Brihaspatir DadhaatuOm Shantih, Shantih, Shantih"

The literal meaning of this mantra is: OM. O Gods! Let us hear auspicious words from our ears. O reverent Gods! Let us behold propitious visions from our eyes, let our organs and body be stable, healthy, and strong. Let us do that which is pleasing to the gods in the life span allotted to us. May Indra, inscribed in the scriptures, bring us fortune! May Pushan, the knower of the world, grant us prosperity! May Trakshya, who vanquishes enemies, bestow us with blessings! May Brihaspati bring us success!
OM Peace, Peace, Peace.

About The Author

Dr. Jagadeesh Pillai is a renowned Guinness World Record holder, writer, and researcher hailing from Varanasi, also known as the abode of Lord Shiva. With a Ph.D. in Vedic Science and a range of creative ideas and achievements, he is a true polymath. He is the author of more than 100 books including Research Publications. Although his roots can be traced back to Kerala, the people of Varanasi hold him in high regard and affectionately consider him one of their own.

In 1998, Dr. Pillai was offered a job at Banaras Hindu University, but he left the position after only two months to pursue greater goals in life. He believed that in order to study Indian scriptures and engage in other creative endeavours, he needed to retire from the daily grind of working solely for money at a young age.

He started an export business from scratch, using the knowledge he had gained from a previous job in the industry. His intelligence and unique approach to business led to great success in a short period of time, earning him more in just a decade and a half than he would have in a lifetime working in a government job. Upon the passing of Dr. APJ Abdul Kalam, Dr. Pillai decided to leave the business and dedicate himself to reading, studying, researching, and experimenting.

During his tenure in the export business, Dr. Pillai traveled to over 16 countries, gaining valuable insight and experiencing the world and life in detail.

Dr. Pillai has achieved four Guinness World Records in the following subjects:

"Script to Screen" - In this record, Dr. Pillai produced and directed an animation film within the shortest time possible, breaking the previous record set by Canadians. He has also received numerous national and international awards and recognitions for this achievement.

Longest Line of Postcards - For this record, Dr. Pillai created a line of 16,300 postcards on the occasion of the 163rd anniversary of Indian Postal Day. The event also included a questionnaire about the Indian flag.

Largest Poster Awareness Campaign - Dr. Pillai designed an awareness campaign on the subject of "Beti Bachao - Beti Padhao" (Save the Girl Child - Educate the Girl Child) to achieve this record.

Largest Envelope - In tribute to the Indian Prime Minister's "Make in India" initiative, Dr. Pillai created a 4000 square meter envelope using waste paper to achieve this record.

Attempted - **70000 Candles on a 210 kg Cake** - To celebrate the 70th Indian Independence Day, Dr. Pillai attempted to light 70,000 candles on a 210 kg cake, which was recorded in World Records India.

Attempted - **Documentary on Dhamek Stupa of Sarnath in 17 Languages** - Dr. Pillai attempted to create a documentary on the Dhamek Stupa of Sarnath, dubbing it in 17 different languages. The result of this attempt is currently awaiting confirmation from the Guinness World Records.

Dr. Pillai is skilled in teaching the Bhagavad Gita, a Hindu scripture, and is popular among young people. He has helped many young people improve their lives through his motivational teachings.

In addition to teaching, he has composed and sung numerous Sanskrit Bhajans and patriotic songs.

He has also written and directed several short films and documentaries for awareness campaigns, and has volunteered with the police in both UP and Kerala to spread awareness about various issues through videos and photography.

Incredibly, he has produced and directed over 100 documentaries about the city of Varanasi, all on his own.

He has also helped and guided more than 25 boys and girls to achieve world records through creative and innovative methods. He is a multifaceted person who uses his intellect and the blessings given to him by God to excel in various areas. He is both a teacher and a student, always learning and teaching, and is able to master any subject he comes across.

He is a selfless social activist and motivational speaker who has overcome struggles and failures to become a successful and enthusiastic individual with a rich life experience.

In addition to his work with the Bhagavad Gita, he is also an efficient Tarot card reader, Astro-Vastu consultant, and a talented singer and composer. He has sung the entire Ram Charita Manas and Bhagavad Gita in his own compositions, and has sung the phrase "Lokah Samastha Sukhino Bhavantu" in 50 different languages. He is currently working on a detailed and scientific study of Vedas, Upanishads, Puranas, and the Bhagavad Gita. He has also composed and sung the Hanuman Chalisa and Gayatri Mantra in 108 and 1008 different compositions, respectively.

Awards - Four Times Guinness World Records, Winner of Mahatma Gandhi Vishwa Shanti Puraskar, Mahatma Gandhi Global Peace Ambassador, Kashi Ratna Award, Dr. APJ Abdul Kalam Motivational Person of the Year 2017, Mother Teresa Award, Indira Gandhi Priyadarshini Award, Bharat Vikas Ratna Award, Udyog Ratna Award, Vigyan Prasar Award, Poorvanchal Ratn Samman.

Preface

India is renowned for its rich and vibrant natural beauty and diversity. This book, The Indian Landscapes and Nature: An Exploration of India's Natural Beauty and Diversity, seeks to explore the country's topographical landscapes, wildlife and marine life, flora and fauna, climate and weather, water resources, mountain ranges, national parks and sanctuaries, protected areas, rivers and lakes, and sustainable development strategies.

This book is intended to serve as an introduction to the rich natural beauty and diversity of India for readers who are new to the subject. It explores India's topographical landscapes, wildlife and marine life, flora and fauna, climate and weather, water resources, mountain ranges, national parks and sanctuaries, protected areas, rivers and lakes, and sustainable development strategies.

The book draws on research from a variety of sources, including interviews with key figures in the Indian environmental community, archival materials, and cultural analysis. I have also conducted extensive field research in India, including visiting parks and reserves, interviewing experts, and visiting locations associated with the production of wildlife conservation and sustainable development initiatives. Through this research, I hope to provide readers with a comprehensive understanding of the Indian environment and its various components.

I am deeply passionate about India's natural beauty and diversity and hope that this book will help to spread the appreciation of this wonderful part of the world. I believe that India has a great deal to offer in terms of its natural beauty and diversity and I am excited to share its cultural and historical significance with my readers.

I

Introduction to India's Natural Beauty and Diversity

India, a land of contrasts and diversity, is home to a wide range of natural landscapes, from majestic mountains and sprawling deserts to lush forests and tropical beaches. From the snow-capped peaks of the Himalayas to the verdant Western Ghats, India's natural beauty is as diverse as its people.

The Himalayas, the world's highest mountain range, dominate the northern region of India and are home to some of the most spectacular landscapes in the country. The towering peaks of Mount Everest and Kanchenjunga, the highest and third-highest peaks in the world respectively, are just two of the many notable peaks that draw mountaineers and trekkers from around the world. The region is also home to a wide variety of flora and fauna, including the endangered snow leopard and the elusive blue sheep.

Further south, the Western Ghats, a UNESCO World Heritage Site, is a mountain range that runs parallel to the western coast of India. The Ghats are known for their rich biodiversity, with a wide variety of plant and animal life, including several endemic species. The region is also home to some of the country's most beautiful waterfalls, such as the Jog Falls and the Dudhsagar Falls, as well as several hill stations, such as Ooty and Munnar, that are popular tourist destinations.

The Thar Desert, also known as the Great Indian Desert, is located in the western part of the country and is one of the driest regions in India. Despite its harsh climate, the desert is home to a variety of plant and animal life, including the iconic Indian camel and the endangered Great Indian Bustard. The desert is also home to several historic forts and palaces, such as the Junagarh Fort and the Mehrangarh Fort, that are popular tourist destinations.

In the east, the Sundarbans, a UNESCO World Heritage Site, is the largest mangrove forest in the world and is home to a wide variety of plant and animal life, including the Bengal tiger, the Indian crocodile and the spotted deer. The forest is also home to several small villages that are inhabited by the indigenous people of the region, who rely on the forest for their livelihood.

The Indian Ocean, which borders the southernmost tip of

India, is home to some of the most beautiful beaches in the country. The beaches, such as the Kovalam Beach and the Varkala Beach, are popular tourist destinations, known for their clear waters and white sandy beaches. The region is also home to several coral reefs and marine life, making it a popular spot for diving and snorkeling.

In this book, we will explore the natural landscapes and diversity of India, from the majestic peaks of the Himalayas to the lush forests of the Western Ghats, and from the deserts of the Thar to the beaches of the Indian Ocean. Through a combination of beautiful photographs and informative text, we will delve into the rich history, culture, and biodiversity of this incredible country, and discover why India truly is a land of contrasts and diversity.

"The beauty of India is not in its monuments, but in its people and their way of life."

ฌ

II

India's Topographical Landscapes

India is a country of diverse landscapes and natural beauty. From the towering Himalayas in the north to the pristine beaches of the south, India offers a wide range of topographical landscapes that are sure to take your breath away.

The Himalayan mountain range, which runs through the northern part of India, is home to some of the highest peaks in the world, including Mount Everest. These majestic mountains offer spectacular views and a wide range of trekking and climbing opportunities for adventure seekers.

Moving down from the mountains, we come to the lush and verdant Indian Plains. This vast expanse of land is home to the country's major river systems, including the Ganges and the Brahmaputra, and is known for its fertile soil and rich agricultural land.

Further south, we find the Deccan Plateau, a large plateau that covers much of South India. This region is known for its rugged terrain, and is home to many of India's ancient temples and monuments.

Finally, we come to the coastal region of India, which is known for its beautiful beaches, lush tropical forests, and a wide range of marine life. The western coast is known for its beaches and the Arabian sea, while the eastern coast is known for its beautiful Bay of Bengal and the Andaman and Nicobar Islands.

In addition to these varied landscapes, India is also home to a wide range of flora and fauna, including many endangered species, making it an important destination for nature lovers and conservationists.

This chapter is just the beginning of a journey through the vast and varied landscapes and natural beauty of India. From the majestic Himalayas to the pristine beaches, India offers an endless array of natural wonders that are sure to leave a lasting impression on all who visit.

"India is not a country, it is a civilization."

- Winston Churchill

ஐ

III

India's Wildlife and Marine Life

India is home to a wide range of wildlife and marine life, making it a paradise for nature enthusiasts and conservationists. The country is home to a diverse array of animals, including the Bengal tiger, Indian elephant, Indian rhinoceros, and Asiatic lion, as well as many species of birds and reptiles.

One of the most iconic animals of India is the Bengal tiger, which is found in the country's national parks and wildlife sanctuaries. The Bengal tiger is an endangered species, and conservation efforts are underway to protect and preserve the remaining population.

Another important animal in India is the Indian elephant, which is also found in the country's national parks and wildlife sanctuaries. The Indian elephant is considered a sacred animal in Hindu culture and is also an important symbol of the country.

In addition to terrestrial wildlife, India also boasts a rich marine life, including the whale shark, saltwater crocodile, and the Ganges river dolphin. The Andaman and Nicobar Islands are known for their coral reefs, and offer great opportunities for diving and snorkeling. The Gulf of Kutch, Gulf of Mannar and the Sundarbans are also rich in marine biodiversity.

India is also home to many national parks and wildlife sanctuaries, such as the Kaziranga National Park, Kanha National Park, and the Sundarbans National Park, which offer visitors the opportunity to see India's wildlife and marine life in their natural habitat.

Conservation efforts are also being made to protect India's wildlife and marine life, as many species are endangered. India's government and various non-profit organizations are working to protect and preserve these animals for future generations to enjoy.

This chapter highlights the rich diversity of India's wildlife and marine life, which is an important aspect of the country's natural beauty. From the Bengal tiger to the Indian elephant, India offers a wide range of wildlife and marine life that is sure to leave a lasting impression on all who visit.

"India is the cradle of the human race, the birthplace of human speech, the mother of history, the grandmother of legend, and the great grandmother of tradition."

- Mark Twain

ဆ

IV

India's Flora and Fauna

India is home to a wide range of flora and fauna, making it a paradise for nature enthusiasts and botanists. The country boasts a diverse array of plant and animal species, many of which are found nowhere else in the world.

One of the most notable aspects of India's flora is its diverse range of forests. From the tropical rainforests of the Western Ghats to the coniferous forests of the Himalayas, India's forests are home to a wide range of plant and animal species. The country's forests also play an important role in maintaining the ecological balance and preserving the biodiversity.

India is also home to a wide range of medicinal plants, many of which are used in traditional Ayurvedic medicine. Some of the most important medicinal plants found in India include turmeric, neem, and tulsi.

In addition to its diverse flora, India is also home to a wide range of fauna. From the Bengal tiger to the Indian elephant, India's wildlife is diverse and unique. The country's national parks and wildlife sanctuaries offer visitors the opportunity to see India's wildlife in their natural habitat.

The country is also home to a wide range of birds, reptiles, and insects. The Great Indian Bustard, the Indian peafowl, and the Asian elephant are some of the commonly seen animals in India. India is also home to many species of reptiles, including the King Cobra and the Indian Python, which are found in the country's forests and swamps.

Conservation efforts are also being made to protect India's flora and fauna, as many species are endangered. India's government and various non-profit organizations are working to protect and preserve these plants and animals for future generations to enjoy.

This chapter highlights the rich diversity of India's flora and fauna, which is an important aspect of the country's natural beauty. From the Western Ghats forests to the Bengal tiger, India offers a wide range of flora and fauna that is sure to leave a lasting impression on all who visit.

"India is the land of dreams and romance, of fabulous wealth and fabulous poverty, of splendor and rags, of palaces and hovels, of famine and pestilence, of genii and giants and Aladdin lamps, of tigers and elephants, the cobra and the jungle, the country of a thousand nations and a hundred tongues, of a thousand religions and two million gods, cradle of the human race, birthplace of human speech, mother of history, grandmother of legend, great grandmother of tradition."

- Mark Twain

ꕥ

V

India's Climate and Weather

India's climate is as diverse as its landscapes and wildlife. The country's vast size and varied topography results in a wide range of weather patterns and temperatures.

The northern region of India experiences a continental climate, with hot summers and cold winters. The Himalayas act as a barrier, protecting this region from the colder winds of Central Asia. The northern plains, which are located in the Gangetic plain, experience extreme temperature variations between winter and summer.

The southern region of India has a tropical climate, with high temperatures and high humidity throughout the year. The coastal areas are influenced by the monsoons, which bring heavy rains during the summer months. The Western Ghats, which run parallel to the western coast of India, act as a barrier, protecting the coast from the monsoons.

The eastern region of India has a tropical climate, with high temperatures and high humidity throughout the year. The region is also influenced by the monsoons, which bring heavy rains during the summer months. The northeastern region of India is also known for receiving heavy rainfall due to its proximity to the Bay of Bengal.

India's climate is also known for its two main seasons: the monsoon season and the dry season. The monsoon season, which starts in June and lasts until September, brings heavy rainfall to much of the country. The dry season, which lasts from October to May, is characterized by low rainfall and high temperatures.

Overall, India's climate and weather is a reflection of its diverse landscapes and topography. The country's varied weather patterns and temperatures offer visitors a wide range of experiences, from the hot and humid tropical climate of the south to the cold and snowy mountains of the north.

"India is the place to find out how much pain, how much violence, and how much insanity a single individual can take and still survive."

- Ryszard Kapuściński

❧

VI

India's Water Resources

India is blessed with a wide variety of water resources, including rivers, lakes, and groundwater. The country's rivers, which are fed by the Himalayan snowmelt and monsoon rains, are an important source of water for irrigation, drinking, and hydroelectric power. The Ganges, Brahmaputra, and Indus rivers are some of the most important and heavily used rivers in the country.

India also has a number of lakes, which are formed by the monsoon rains and river floods. Many of these lakes are important sources of water for irrigation and drinking, and they also serve as habitats for a wide variety of aquatic life. The Wular Lake in Jammu and Kashmir and the Chilika Lake in Odisha are among the largest and most important lakes in India.

Groundwater is also an important source of water for India.

The country has a large number of aquifers, which are underground layers of water-bearing rock. These aquifers can be tapped using wells and boreholes, providing a reliable source of water for irrigation and drinking.

In addition to these traditional water resources, India is also investing in modern water management techniques such as rainwater harvesting, desalination, and water recycling. These techniques can help to conserve and manage the country's water resources more efficiently.

Despite the abundance of water resources in India, the country still faces water scarcity and water-related challenges. Climate change, population growth, and pollution are putting pressure on the country's water resources. The government of India has undertaken several initiatives to conserve water, such as the National Water Policy and the National River Conservation Plan, which aim to promote sustainable water management practices and protect the country's water resources.

Overall, India's water resources are an important asset for the country and its people. With proper management and conservation, these resources can continue to support the country's economic development and improve the lives of its citizens.

"India is the land of noble traditions, where the past blends with the present to create a unique cultural heritage."

ཀ

VII

India's Mountain Ranges

India is home to a number of majestic mountain ranges, each with their own unique beauty and characteristics. The most prominent of these is the Himalayas, which stretch across northern India and include some of the highest peaks in the world, including Mount Everest. The Himalayas are known for their stunning snow-capped peaks, glaciers, and alpine meadows, and are popular for trekking, climbing, and skiing.

Another important mountain range in India is the Western Ghats, which runs parallel to the western coast of India. These mountains are known for their lush tropical forests, waterfalls, and rich biodiversity. The Western Ghats are home to many endangered species, including the Asian elephant, tiger, and leopard. They are also an important source of water for the surrounding regions and are designated as a UNESCO World Heritage Site.

The Eastern Ghats, located on the eastern coast of India, is a range of mountains that are not as well-known as the Western Ghats, but they are still an important ecological and cultural feature of the region. They are known for their beautiful waterfalls, hill stations and ancient temples.

The Aravalli Range, located in the western part of India, is one of the oldest mountain ranges in the world. It is known for its rocky terrain, ancient temples, and historic forts.

The Satpura Range, located in the central part of India, is known for its dense forests, waterfalls, and wildlife. The range is also home to a number of tribal communities, who have lived in harmony with the forest for centuries.

Overall, India's mountain ranges offer a wide range of natural beauty and adventure opportunities for visitors, as well as providing ecological and cultural significance to the country. The government of India has also taken some initiative to protect these mountain ranges and their biodiversity, by creating national park and wildlife sanctuary.

"India is a land of contrasts, where ancient traditions and modern technology coexist in harmony."

VIII

India's National Parks and Sanctuaries

India is home to a diverse range of wildlife, and as a result, it is also home to a number of national parks and wildlife sanctuaries that aim to protect and conserve the country's unique flora and fauna. Some of the most famous and popular national parks and sanctuaries in India include:

Kanha National Park: Located in the state of Madhya Pradesh, Kanha National Park is known for its large population of Bengal tigers, as well as for its picturesque meadows and forests.

Sundarbans National Park: Located in the state of West Bengal, Sundarbans National Park is a UNESCO World Heritage Site and is known for its large population of Bengal tigers, as well as for its mangrove forests and unique ecosystem.

Gir National Park: Located in the state of Gujarat, Gir National Park is the only place in the world where Asiatic lions can be found in the wild. The park is also home to a wide range of other wildlife, including leopards, crocodiles, and over 300 species of birds.

Ranthambore National Park: Located in the state of Rajasthan, Ranthambore National Park is known for its large population of Bengal tigers and is a popular spot for wildlife safaris.

Kaziranga National Park: Located in the state of Assam, Kaziranga National Park is a UNESCO World Heritage Site and is known for its large population of one-horned rhinoceroses, as well as for its elephant and buffalo populations.

Corbett National Park: Located in the state of Uttarakhand, Corbett National Park is India's first national park and is known for its large population of Bengal tigers and leopards, as well as for its diverse range of flora and fauna.

These national parks and sanctuaries, along with many other, not only protect and conserve India's unique wildlife, but also offer visitors the opportunity to experience and appreciate the country's natural beauty and diversity.

"India is a melting pot of cultures, religions, languages, and traditions."

ꕥ

IX

India's Protected Areas

In addition to national parks and wildlife sanctuaries, India also has a number of protected areas that are managed by the government for conservation and preservation of the country's natural resources. These include:

Wildlife Sanctuaries: India has over 500 wildlife sanctuaries that provide protection to a wide range of species, including tigers, elephants, rhinos, and many more.

Biosphere Reserves: India has 18 biosphere reserves, which are designated by UNESCO to promote conservation and sustainable development. These reserves protect large areas of natural ecosystems and provide a balance between conservation and economic development.

Conservation Reserves: India has 45 conservation reserves, which are protected areas that are managed for the conservation of specific species or ecosystems.

Community Reserves: India has 4 community reserves, which are protected areas managed by local communities in partnership with the government.

Marine Protected Areas: India has 14 marine protected areas, which are designated to protect and conserve the country's marine and coastal ecosystems.

These protected areas, along with the national parks and wildlife sanctuaries, play a crucial role in protecting and preserving India's diverse natural heritage and biodiversity. They also provide opportunities for ecotourism, research, and education, and help to promote conservation and sustainable development across the country.

Overall, India's protected areas offer diverse landscapes, climate, and ecosystems, which provide a wide variety of opportunities for visitors to experience and appreciate India's natural beauty and diversity.

"India is where spirituality and materialism coexist in perfect balance."

X

India's Rivers and Lakes

India is home to a diverse range of rivers and lakes, each with their own unique characteristics and ecological importance. Some of the major rivers in India include:

The Ganges: Known as the "holy river" to Hindus, the Ganges is the longest river in India and one of the most sacred in Hinduism. It flows through northern India and Bangladesh, and is considered to be the lifeline of millions of people living along its banks.

The Brahmaputra: The Brahmaputra is one of the largest rivers in Asia, flowing through China, India, and Bangladesh. It is known for its wide and braided channels, and is home to a diverse range of fish and aquatic species.

The Godavari: The Godavari is the second longest river in India, flowing through the states of Maharashtra, Andhra

Pradesh, and Telangana. It is considered to be one of the most sacred rivers in India and is home to a number of important pilgrimage sites.

The Yamuna: The Yamuna is a major tributary of the Ganges, flowing through the states of Uttarakhand, Haryana, and Uttar Pradesh. It is considered to be one of the most polluted rivers in India due to the large amount of industrial and agricultural waste that is dumped into it.

The Narmada: The Narmada is one of the few major rivers in India that flows westwards, originating from the Amarkantak plateau in Madhya Pradesh. It is also considered as one of the seven most sacred rivers in Hinduism.

In addition to rivers, India also has a number of significant lakes, such as the Wular lake, Chilika lake, and Vembanad lake, which are known for their unique biodiversity, water-based activities, and scenic beauty.

Overall, India's rivers and lakes play a vital role in the country's economy and ecology, providing water for irrigation, hydropower, and drinking, as well as habitat for a diverse range of fish and aquatic species. They also provide a rich cultural and spiritual significance and contribute to India's natural beauty and diversity.

"India is a land of diversity, where every state and region has its own unique culture and traditions."

ꟷ

XI

Sustainable Development in India

India is home to a diverse and unique natural landscape, with a wide range of topographical features, wildlife, flora, and fauna. From the snow-capped peaks of the Himalayas to the tropical beaches of the south, India's natural beauty is truly breathtaking.

The country's wildlife and marine life is also diverse, with a wide range of animals and marine creatures that are found only in India. The country's flora and fauna are also rich and varied, with many species that are found only in India.

India's climate and weather are also diverse, with different regions experiencing different types of weather conditions. The country's water resources are also diverse and range from rivers, lakes, and wetlands to ground water, and these resources are essential for the survival of the country's wildlife and human population.

India is also home to several mountain ranges, including the Himalayas, the Western Ghats, and the Eastern Ghats. These mountain ranges are not only home to a wide range of flora and fauna, but they also provide important ecological services to the country.

India also boasts of several national parks and sanctuaries, which are home to a wide range of wildlife and are an important part of the country's natural heritage. These protected areas are important for the conservation of the country's wildlife, and for the enjoyment of visitors.

India's rivers and lakes also play an important role in the country's ecology, culture, and economy. Many of the country's rivers are considered sacred by the local population and are an important source of water for irrigation, drinking, and hydroelectric power.

The country has made significant strides in sustainable development, with the government and other organizations implementing various policies and initiatives to promote sustainable development in different sectors. These include initiatives in the areas of renewable energy, green transportation, and sustainable tourism.

In conclusion, India's natural beauty and diversity are truly awe-inspiring and an important part of the country's cultural and economic heritage. It is essential that we take steps to preserve and protect these resources for future generations to enjoy.

"India is a land of beauty, from the majestic Himalayas to the tranquil backwaters of Kerala."

XII

Kashmir to Kanyakumari

India is a country rich in natural beauty and resources, spanning from the snow-capped Himalayas in the north to the tropical beaches of the south. The diversity of landscapes and ecosystems in India is truly remarkable, ranging from lush rainforests to arid deserts, and from tranquil lakes to fast-flowing rivers.

In the northern region of Kashmir, the Himalayan mountain range provides a stunning backdrop for the region's alpine meadows and glistening glaciers. The region is also home to a wide variety of wildlife, including the endangered snow leopard and the Himalayan black bear.

Moving further south, the Western Ghats mountain range is a biodiversity hotspot, with a wide variety of endemic species of plants and animals. The region also boasts of several national parks and wildlife sanctuaries, such as the

Periyar National Park, which is known for its elephant population and the Nilgiri Biosphere Reserve, which is home to the Bengal tiger and Indian leopard.

The Deccan Plateau, located in the south-central region of India, is characterized by its rolling hills and dry, scrubby landscapes. The region is known for its rich cultural heritage and historic monuments, such as the Ajanta and Ellora caves, as well as its vibrant wildlife, including the Indian bison and the blackbuck.

Further south, the state of Tamil Nadu is home to the lush, tropical region of the Western Ghats. The region is known for its beautiful beaches, such as the Marina Beach and the Kanyakumari Beach, as well as its rich marine life, including the endangered dugong and the Indian ocean humpback dolphin.

Overall, India's natural beauty and resources are incredibly diverse and offer something for everyone, from the rugged landscapes of the Himalayas to the tropical beaches of the south. The country is also known for its rich biodiversity, with a wide variety of wildlife and plant species, and a range of protected areas and national parks to explore.

"India is a land of ancient wisdom, where spirituality and philosophy have flourished for centuries."

ꕥ

OTHER BOOKS OF THE AUTHOR

1. The Moments When I Met God
2. Kashiyile Theertha Pathangal
3. GURU GYAN VANI
4. Abhiprerak Gita
5. ASSI SE JAIN GHAT TAK
6. Hopelessness of Arjuna
7. The Soul and It's True Nature
8. Sense of Action (Karma)
9. Action through Wisdom
10. Action through Wisdom
11. THEORY AND PRACTICAL OF EVERY ACTION
12. LOGICAL UNDERSTANDING OF THE SUPREME
13. THE IMPERISHABLE SUPREME
14. Yatra Nishadraj se Hanuman Ghat Tak
15. Yatra Karnatak Ghat se Raja Ghat Tak
16. Yatra Pandey Ghat se Prayagraj Ghat Tak
17. Yatra Ranjendra Prasad Ghat se Dattatreya Ghat Tak
18. YaatraSindhiya Ghat se Gwaliar Ghat Tak
19. Yatra Mangala Gauri Ghat se Hanuman Gadhi Ghat Tak
20. Yatra Gaay Ghat Se Nishad Ghat Tak
21. MAA GANGA, GHATEN EVM UTSAV
22. Ganga Arti Dev Deepavali evam Any Utsav
23. Potentials of Digitalized India
24. VEDIC CONSCIOUSNESS
25. A Brief Introduction to Vedic Science
26. Kashi ke Barah Jyotirling
27. IMPACT OF MOTIVATION
28. Let's have a Milky Way Journey
29. Color Therapy in a Nutshell

30. Rigveda in a Nutshell
31. Yajurveda in a Nutshell
32. Samveda in a Nutshell
33. Atharva Veda in a Nutshell
34. Ayushman Bhava - Ayurveda
35. Srimad Bhagavad Gita and Upanishad Connection
36. Srimad Bhagavad Gita - an attempt to summarize each chapter.
37. Facts and Impact of Nakshatra
38. Astro Gems - NAVARATNA
39. Ekadashi - A Concise Overview
40. A Concise View of Hanuman Chalisa
41. Inspirational Gita
42. Nakshatraranyam
43. Summary of 18 Mahapuranas
44. Synopsis of 18 Upa Puranas
45. Rigvediya Upanishads
46. Shukla Yajurvediya Upanishads
47. Krishna Yajurvediya Upanishads
48. Samavediya Upanishads
49. Atharvavediya Upanishads
50. The Seven Great Sages
51. From Rocket Scientist to President Dr. APJ Abdul Kalam
52. The Visionary's Voice - Quotes of Dr. APJ Abdul Kalam
53. The Wisdom of Swami Vivekananda: Insights and Inspiration from a Legendary Spiritual Teacher
54. Ayurvedic Remedies from the Garden
55. Sages and Seers
56. Rising Strong – Motivational Stories of Women
57. Beyond Flames -Mystery stories of Funeral Ghat Manikarnika
58. The Origins of Tulsi: A Look at the Mythological Roots of the Plant"

59. The Holistic Cow: A Look at the Physical, Spiritual, and Cultural Importance of Cows in India
60. Arts of Healing
61. Exploring the Divine
62. Understanding Five Elements
63. The Etymology of Ram
64. Symbols of India
65. Voice of Change (About Speeches of Great Men)
66. She Speaks (About Speeches of Great Women)
67. Patriotism on Celluloid – Brief About Patriotic Films
68. The Music of Motivation: A Brief Guide to Inspirational Film Songs
69. **Unlocking the Secrets of the Dashopanishads**
70. A Cultural Mosaic
71. Ancient Traditions, Modern Minds
72. Ecos of Ancient Wisdom
73. Beneath the Surface
74. From Temples to Ashrams
75. Sages of the Subcontinent
76. The Art of Healling (Ayurveda, Yoga & Naturopathy)
77. Indian Kitchen
78. The Festivals of India
79. The Indian Epics Retold
80. The Power of Mantras
81. The Indian River Ganges
82. The Indian Architecture
83. Rites of Passage
84. The Indian Silk Road
85. The Indian Literature
86. The Indian Villages
87. The Indian Folks & Crafts
88. The Way of Buddha
89. The Ramayan of Tulsidas

90. Astrological Remedies
91. The Secret Power of Motivation
92. Secret of Developing your Inner Strength
93. The Secret Path to Motivation
94. The Art and Secret of Positive Thinking
95. The Secrets of Practicing Ethical Living
96. Indian Art and Painting
97. The Indian Herbalism
98. Bharatanatyam to Kathak
99. Exploring India's Astrological Remedies
100. The Indian Festival of Flowers
101. Indian Handicrafts
102. The Splashes of Joy – India's Colour Festival
103. The Indian Science of Astrology
104. The Indian Mythology
105. Path to Enlightenment
106. The Indian Spirituality for Children
107. Aromas of India
108. The Secrets of Healthy Relationships
109. Ancestral Ties
110. The Indian Street Food
111. Discovering America
112. The Indian Textile
113. Listening to Motivational Speeches
114. Taste of India
115. A Cultural Journey through Indian Nuptials
116. Motivational Quote for Change
117. Secret Strategies for Making Money
118. Secrets to Cultivate a Positive Mindset
119. A Tapestry of Cultures: Exploring India from Kashmir to Kanyakumari
120. Achieving Your Dreams with Resilience: Secret Strategies for Overcoming Obstacles

121. Innovative Startups - 25 Startup Ideas to Spark Your Business Creativity
122. Export Management: Strategies for Global Success
123. Exporting from India - A Step by Step Guide
124. Finance Fundamentals: Mastering Financial Management for Business Success
125. Global Growth Strategies for International Business Development
126. Marketing Mastery: Unlocking the Secrets of Modern Marketing
127. Operations Mastery: Managing the Flow of Value in Business
128. Strategic Business Management: Navigating the Modern Business Landscape
129. Human Resource Management Strategies for Building and Managing a High Performance Team
130. The Indian Landscapes And Nature: An Exploration Of India's Natural Beauty And Diversity

Contact

DR. JAGADEESH PILLAI

MBA & PhD in Vedic Science

Four Times Guinness World Record Holder

Winner of Mahatma Gandhi Vishwa Shanti Puraskar and Global Peace Ambassador

Gemology, Astro & Vastu Consultant - Spiritual Counselor

Consultant for designing World Record Ideas

Efficient Tarot Card Reader

9839093003

myrichindia@gmail.com

drjagadeeshpillai@facebook

drjagadeeshpillai@instagram

jagadeeshpillai@youtube

www. JAGADEESHPILLAI.com

|| LOKAHA SAMASTHAHA SUKHINO BHAVANTU ||

9 798889 591221

Printed by Libri Plureos GmbH in Hamburg,
Germany